ideals®
EASTER

More Than 50 Years of Celebrating Life's Most Treasured Moments
Vol. 54, No. 1

*"The seed of God stirred, shoved, and sprouted.
The ground trembled, and the rock of the tomb
tumbled. And the flower of Easter blossomed."*
—Max L. Lucado

IDEALS—Vol. 54, No. 1 January MCMXCVII IDEALS (ISSN 0019-137X) is published six times a year: January, March,
May, July, September, and November by IDEALS PUBLICATIONS INCORPORATED,
535 Metroplex Drive, Suite 250, Nashville, TN 37211.
Periodical postage paid at Nashville, Tennessee, and additional mailing offices.
Copyright © MCMXCVII by IDEALS PUBLICATIONS INCORPORATED.
POSTMASTER: Send address changes to Ideals, PO Box 305300, Nashville, TN 37230. All rights reserved.
Title IDEALS registered U.S. Patent Office.

SINGLE ISSUE—U.S. $5.95 USD; Higher in Canada
ONE-YEAR SUBSCRIPTION—U.S. $19.95 USD; Canada $36.00 CDN (incl. GST and shipping); Foreign $25.95 USD
TWO-YEAR SUBSCRIPTION—U.S. $35.95 USD; Canada $66.50 CDN (incl. GST and shipping); Foreign $47.95 USD

Subscribers may call customer service at 1-800-558-4343 to make address changes.
Unsolicited manuscripts will not be returned without a self-addressed, stamped envelope.

ISBN 0-8249-1134-2   GST 131903775

Cover Photo
LILIES FOR EASTER
Norman Poole Photography

Inside Covers
ANTIQUE EASTER CARDS
Superstock

D0131541

Easter
in New England
Rose Koralewsky

There is no death! Life is triumphant as ever!
Though wintry gales still sweep across the plain,
Though drifts still lurk unmelted on the mountains
And blue spring skies grow dark with sleet and rain,

Forsythia drips with gold despite the snowflakes,
And violets wink bright eyes mid whitened grass;
The robin's carol yields not to the tempest;
The bluebird murmurs that this too will pass.

Perennial miracle of Life's renewal,
How manifest to us this holy day!
Again we stand in silence and in wonder,
And from our hearts the stone is rolled away.

Renewal
Kay Hoffman

Weary of winter's lingering day,
I walked along an old pathway.
Sullen and bare were the trees and sod;
There seemed so little here to laud.

Then mid snowflakes, a lacy few,
I saw a crocus pushing through;
And in a treetop veiled with haze,
A robin sang his morning praise.

My thoughts turned to our caring God
Who puts the crocus in the sod
And lifts the small bird's heart to sing
At the first faint hint of spring.

I brushed snowflakes from crocus there
And humbly bowed in praise and prayer;
God had sent His spring anew
And in my heart renewal too.

CROCUS WITH LATE SPRING SNOW
Corvallis, Oregon
Dennis Frates/Oregon Scenics

The Waking Year

Emily Dickinson

A lady red upon the hill
　　Her annual secret keeps;
A lady white within the field
　　In placid lily sleeps!

The tidy breezes with their brooms
　　Sweep vale, and hill, and tree;
Prithee, my pretty housewives,
　　Who may expected be?

The neighbors do not yet suspect,
　　The woods exchange a smile—
Orchard and buttercup and bird—
　　In such a little while!

And yet how still the landscape stands,
　　How nonchalant the wood,
As if the resurrection
　　Were nothing very odd!

Eastertime

Virginia Borman Grimmer

Now comes spring and Eastertime;
　　What a cause for lilting rhyme,
When the earth from winter's nap
　　Sheds somber shawl for bright green wrap
While busy birds weave tidy nests
　　With flapping wings and dipping crests
And skies send down soft, gentle rains
　　As Nature hums her sweet refrains.
Then sunshine melts away the snows
　　Till rivulets run on in rows
As crocus nod their little heads,
　　The first to rise in sheltered beds.
For it is spring, and once again
　　Warmth rests upon the hill and glen;
And all the freshness of the earth
　　Tells of newness and rebirth.
For it is Eastertime so grand,
　　And resurrection's on the land.

As Spring Unfolds

Rebecca Wells

Unfolding now before my eyes
In panoramic view
Is springtime in arrival stage,
All wondrous, fresh, and new.

The willows first announce the change
In wispy, pale green hue;
And after winter's brutal force,
It seems long overdue.

Too slow at first the leaves unfold;
But then the Master's hand

Just touches them and they explode,
Revealing beauty grand.

In shades of green, magnificent,
Each shade a true delight,
The flow'ring trees, with fragrance sweet,
Add red and pink and white.

I watch, and as the view unfolds,
My eyes dance at the scene;
In gratitude I bow to Him
For springtime's gift of green.

A Rare Gift

Verna Sparks

He who has a garden
Has treasures to behold,
A workshop for his conscience,
A place to dig for gold,
A pleasure and a profit
And happiness combined;
A garden is the rarest gift
That anyone can find.

Spring

Herman T. Roberts

Spring has brought such lovely things—
　　Daffodils, triumphant wings,
Crocus blossoms, seeds with hopes,
　　Clover strewn on emerald slopes,
April showers that lightly kissed
　　Beds of pink and amethyst.
When she woke from mystic dreams,
　　Wearing robes of bright sunbeams,
Spring stepped out with merry air,
　　Spreading beauty everywhere.
And when Jesus, from the grave,
　　Rose triumphantly, He gave
Hope and faith; and they shall bring
　　Joy as wonderful as spring.

SPRING TULIPS
Ottawa, Ontario
Josiah Davidson Scenic Photography

Overleaf Photograph
LUPINE AND BISTORT
Mt. Rainier National Park, Washington
Adam Jones Photography

Readers' Reflections

Editor's Note: Readers are invited to submit unpublished, original poetry for possible publication in future issues of Ideals. Please send typed copies only; manuscripts will not be returned. Writers receive $10 for each published submission. Send material to Readers' Reflections, Ideals Publications Inc., 535 Metroplex Drive, Suite 250, Nashville, Tennessee 37211.

CLOUDS

If I had a net
    Like some fishermen do,
I would cast it up high
    Into skies oh so blue.
No catch would be
    Too large or too small;
White clouds or dark clouds—
    I would keep them all.

I would stand in the market
    And give up my wares.
There would be a small charge:
    A list of your cares.
I would bag up fluffy, white clouds
    For sought-after dreamers,
A few scattered gray ones
    For dubious schemers,

Display baskets of pink ones
    For charmers, who cannot abstain;
No shortage of black clouds
    For farmers, who might need the rain.
The clouds with silver linings
    Would be in such demand;
Bits of silver-filled fluff
    Would fill each empty hand.

When the market is closed
    At the end of the day,
I would hang up my apron—
    The catch all given away.
And while nearby sellers
    Dropped coins into jars,
I would reach for my net
    And go for the stars.

C. Haney
New Brunswick, Canada

GOD'S FLOWER

I'm just a little flower
That's blooming here for God,
Although the other folks around
May think that I am odd.

I cannot sing great operas;
My voice is only fair.
But if I bring a song to one,
I'm glad that I was there.

I seldom know what's proper
To say to one in pain;
But if I give a clasp or hug,
I have not passed in vain.

I'm just a little flower;
That's all I'll ever be.
But if that's good enough for God,
It's good enough for me.

Sherrie Ferens
Kettering, Ohio

LEGACY

If I should plant a lilac bush
And know right from the start
I'll never smell its fragrant scent
Before I must depart;
Or plant a mighty oak tree
And know one thing for certain,
I'll never rest beneath its shade
Before that final curtain;
And if someone else can know
The joy of beauty I have given,
Then I know I've learned the secret
Of a wondrous way of living.
For if the sunset comes too soon
Upon the earth you've trod,
And you've sown a little happiness,
You've walked closer with your God.

Marion I. Kaufman
Fond du Lac, Wisconsin

APRIL

Rose-gold is the glow of evening now.
Robin sings on apple bough;
Stars twinkle down through the soft, velvet night;
Little, round Moon bathes earth with her light.
Rain fills the tulips in the cool, dewy morn,
And all creation is newly born.
Flower-time, bird-time—
These lovely things.
My soul laughs and soars and sings!

J. Myers
Cincinnati, Ohio

SPRING

The robin's back,
The snow is gone,
The grass is new and green.
Our hearts are full of joy today;
Welcome, welcome, Spring!

Vickie Riley
North Little Rock, Arkansas

Springtime Breeze

Beverly J. Anderson

Carefree, gentle springtime breeze
Whisp'ring to the new-clad trees
Bids the birds to wake and sing
Joyful songs because it's spring.
Bending low, you touch each flower,
Telling them now is the hour
For their petals to unfold;
Spring has broken winter's hold.

Mauves and pinks and golds and reds
Raise their pretty, ornate heads.
Then from every scented bloom,
You scoop up their sweet perfume.
Springtime breeze, you fill the air,
Spilling fragrance everywhere.
Spring has come! Wake from your dream!
You tell every brook and stream.

Soon the earth is stirred anew.
Chicks and bunnies appear too.
Little children laugh and shout
As they toss their kites about.
Playful breeze, you skip along
To the beat of springtime's song;
And atop the greening hills,
There you waltz with daffodils.

AZALEA WOODS
Winterthur Gardens, Delaware
Gene Ahrens Photography

THIS IS EASTER

When Easter follows along in the footsteps of spring's arrival, I always feel that the vernal season is more sure of herself. Even I feel more confident and sure.

The spring warmth began moving in weeks ago. The sun is higher, warmer, more kind. Grass grows and greens. So do the grains. The flowers come. Birds are nesting. I have the bluebirds and chickadees, the wrens and titmice in my dooryard boxes. Cardinals and towhees are nesting in the hedges. The ground-nesters seek the pastures and fields, the redwings seek the thickets in the marsh.

It is time to start my daily walks once more. I neglected them for most of the winter, those days of snow and cold and biting winds. Spring will walk with me today, I am sure, through the glorious countryside of South Carolina.

I love to see and hear the babbling brook purling around the stones, so first I follow the stream in the woodland. The delicate blossoms of the pinxter bush fill the air with richness and fragrance. Then I meander down to the pasture where cat-tle graze in the peace and contentment of the outdoor world. I walk to the marsh where the redwings play their flutes and where the turtles sun themselves on fallen logs. I am mesmerized by the ripples left behind as muskrats and beaver swim in the warming channel of the stream.

This is Easter. Life is reborn, renewed, and we are filled with faith and hope. We rejoice in our trust of eternal life. We see it in nature, and we feel it within our souls.

Rejoice! Sing from the highest hill. Sing your glory to God. You see the new leaves come, the buds, the flowers. You hear the songs. You sense the rebirth of nature within your being. And you sing of it within your heart.

The author of two published books, Lansing Christman has been contributing to Ideals for more than twenty years. Mr. Christman has also been published in several American, foreign, and braille anthologies. He lives in rural South Carolina.

From the Redwoods

Minnie Klemme

In the temple of the redwoods
    Where the spires touch the sky,
Where the tall winds play the organ
    And the mists come rolling by,

There God daily holds communion
    With His creatures great and small.
There I paused one day to listen;
    There I heard God's altar call.

In the ancient redwood forests,
    In creation's timeless way,
Still the ages keep their altars
    That the world may learn to pray.

from A Forest Hymn

William Cullen Bryant

The groves were God's first temples. Ere man learned
To hew the shaft, and lay the architrave,
And spread the roof above them—ere he framed
The lofty vault, to gather and roll back
The sound of anthems; in the darkling wood,
Amid the cool and silence, he knelt down
And offered to the Mightiest solemn thanks
And supplication.

RHODODENDRON
Redwood National Park, California
Dennis Frates/Oregon Scenics

From My Garden Journal

by Deana Deck

DAFFODIL

One of the most romantic gifts I ever received was a daffodil in a soda pop bottle. I was a young college student working in a gift shop between classes. My friend Jimmy, perennially short on funds as we all were in those days, frequently walked to campus in good weather and often stopped by the shop to visit. On this day in early May, far north where it doesn't quit snowing until mid-May and most flowers don't venture out until Memorial Day, Jimmy had spotted a wild daffodil growing beside the road and brought it to me in an old soda pop bottle. He handed it to me with a sweet smile, and spring happened.

No matter when they bloom or what the climate, daffodils are a universal symbol of spring. Until the daffodils appear, spring hasn't really begun. In fact, ask someone to name a spring flower and chances are *daffodil* will be one of the first words that come to mind.

Daffodils belong to the large family of spring-flowering bulb plants with the species name *narcissus*. Therefore, all daffodils are narcissus, although not all narcissus are daffodils. The narcissus species is divided into twelve classes, one of which is the Trumpet, the classic form we usually picture when we think of daffodils. Other classes or divisions include those with double blossoms, large cups, short cups, and similar variations.

Nurseries today offer vast numbers of multi-colored, multi-flowered, ruffled daffodils developed in recent years by commercial bulb growers around the world, primarily in England and Ireland. In the United States, many new varieties have been developed in Oregon.

Holland is still a source for daffodils as well; and Dutch bulbs, grown mostly for cutting and naturalizing, are usually the ones offered in mail-order catalogs. Bulbs from England, Ireland, and Oregon are more expensive; but they are specimen quality and are grown for the perfection of the bloom. More and more gardeners are choosing these bulbs due to their vibrant, uniquely colored flowers and the interesting varieties available, such as the "butterflies" (which sport split, ruffled crowns), the yellow-to-pink Amber Castle, and the white and red Woodland Star.

If you picture your spring garden brimming with these more interesting types of daffodils, it's a good idea to order early and in bulk. Because growers won't accept small orders from garden centers, most centers only carry the most popular, well-known varieties to avoid large quantities of unsold, expensive bulbs. If several neighbors or a garden club is interested in a hard-to-find or unusual daffodil variety, most dealers will place a large order for them.

Selection is best in August when bulbs first begin arriving at garden centers. If you live in a northern climate, this date poses no problem; just plant your bulbs in September or October. The further south you live, however, the later you should plant, because bulbs planted when the soil is too warm tend to sprout too early and are damaged in the first cold spell. In the deepest south, gardeners often purchase their bulbs at the end of summer but must store them in the vegetable bin of the refrigerator until late November or early December, when the soil has cooled enough for planting. I keep an old refrigerator in my potting shed specifically for storing seeds and bulbs.

Daffodils look most brilliant and are easier to plant in drifts, rather than formal, single-file lines. Dig out the bed to a depth of twelve inches. To the removed soil, add builder's sand to encourage draining, compost for nitrogen, bone meal or bulb food for root and bloom development, and dry peat moss. Return a six-inch layer of the mix to the bed, set the bulbs onto this layer (pointed side up), cover with the rest of the soil mix, and water well. This method is much more practical than digging a hole for every plant, especially if you're planting a hundred or more bulbs!

One of the advantages of all bulbs is their "plant it and forget it" quality. When planted in a well prepared bed, bulbs require little maintenance since they contain everything they need to grow and bloom. After the first year, however,

Some species of daffodil can be forced to bloom indoors. Place your potted bulbs in a sunny windowsill and soon spring will brighten your window.

the plants will benefit from a spring dose of 0-20-20 fertilizer or bone meal as soon as the foliage tips appear and once more in the fall. During the active growing season, bulbs require watering if spring rains are light. Mulch the bulbs with wood ashes from the fireplace in the winter.

Daffodils multiply quickly; within a few years, a garden started with just a few handfuls of bulbs will contain dozens of beautiful plants. For healthy, vigorously blooming plants, divide bulbs every five years. When dividing, allow them to dry for a few days. Then brush the dirt off gently and dust each bulb with benomyl, a fungicide that prevents bulb rot.

In the south, daffodils can appear as early as Valentine's Day; the further north you go, the later they will bloom. But one thing is certain: after you see the first daffodil break through the cold earth, you can relax. Spring has come around again. It is time once more to fill a vase, or even an old soda pop bottle, with the sunshine brightness of the daffodil.

Deana Deck tends to her flowers, plants, and vegetables at her home in Nashville, Tennessee, where her popular garden column is a regular feature in The Tennessean.

BITS & PIECES

I'd be a butterfly born in a bow'r,
  Where roses and lilies and violets meet.
  —*Thomas Haynes Bayly*

*S*pringtime . . . invites you to try out its splendor . . .
to believe anew, to realize that the same Lord who
renews the trees with buds and blossoms is ready to
renew your life with hope and courage.
  —*Charles R. Swindoll*

*S*pring . . . it is a natural resurrection,
  an experience of immortality.
  —*Henry David Thoreau*

*S*pring unlocks the flowers to paint the laughing soil.
  —*Reginald Heber*

With the rose the butterfly's deep in love,
A thousand times hovering round;
But round himself all tender like gold,
The sun's sweet ray is hovering found.
—*Heine*

Every April, God rewrites the book of Genesis.
—*Author Unknown*

As the dewdrops shimmer on the wings of the butterfly,
my heart smiles to know the promise of spring is fulfilled.
—*Author Unknown*

Happiness is as a butterfly, which, when pursued,
is always just beyond our grasp, but which, if you
will sit down quietly, may alight upon you.
—*Nathaniel Hawthorne*

Kite Tale

Nancy Allan

I tie my troubles to a kite
And watch till they are out of sight—
A litany of slights and hurts
Tied to a kite that dips and flirts
With trees and clouds and telephone wire,
Stopping to chat with an old church spire.
Resting its head on a grand blue sky,
It suddenly begins to fly,
Its tail a speck from down below.
I open my hand and let it go.

The Kite String

Erma L. Stull

One windy day a tow-haired boy
Was happily sailing his kite;
He scampered on, and soon the breeze
Had lifted it out of his sight.

Although unseen in its drifting,
No fear crossed the face of the boy;
Then his dad, thinking it broken,
Asked, "Son, have you lost your new toy?"

But the lad just grinned and replied,
"You can't see it, but one sure thing:
I'm positive that it's still there
'Cause I feel the pull of the string."

Except we become as this child,
We shall miss the truth he imparts.
Unseen, unheard, we know God's near
When we feel Him tug at our hearts.

24

KITE FLYING DAYS
Jacob Taposchaner
FPG International

FOR THE CHILDREN

THE MOON'S THE NORTH WIND'S COOKY

Vachel Lindsay

The Moon's the North Wind's cooky.
   He bites it, day by day,
Until there's but a rim of scraps
   That crumble all away.

The South Wind is a baker.
   He kneads clouds in his den
And bakes a crisp new moon *that . . . greedy*
   North . . . Wind . . . eats . . . again!

THE SENSES: SEEING
Jessie Wilcox Smith, artist
Fine Art Photographic Library Ltd.

OUR HERITAGE

FROM *PAUL REVERE'S RIDE*

Henry Wadsworth Longfellow

Listen, my children, and you shall hear
Of the midnight ride of Paul Revere
On the eighteenth of April, in seventy-five;
Hardly a man is now alive
Who remembers that famous day and year.

He said to his friend, "If the British march
By land or sea from town tonight,
Hang a lantern aloft in the belfry arch
Of the North Church tower as a signal light—
One, if by land, and two, if by sea;
And I on the opposite shore will be,
Ready to ride and spread the alarm
Through every Middlesex village and farm
For the country folk to be up and to arm."

Then he said, "Good night!" and with muffled oar
Silently rowed to the Charleston shore. . . .

Meanwhile, his friend, through alley and street,
Wanders and watches with eager ears,
Till in the silence around him he hears
The muster of men at the barrack door,
The sound of arms, and the tramp of feet,
And the measured tread of the grenadiers
Marching down to their boats on the shore.

Meanwhile, impatient to mount and ride,
Booted and spurred, with a heavy stride
On the opposite shore walked Paul Revere.
And lo! as he looks on the belfry's height
A glimmer, and then a gleam of light!
He springs to the saddle, the bridle he turns,
But lingers and gazes, till full on his sight
A second lamp in the belfry burns!

It was twelve by the village clock,
When he crossed the bridge into Medford town.
He heard the crowing of the cock
And the barking of the farmer's dog
And felt the damp of the river fog
That rises after the sun goes down.

It was one by the village clock
When he galloped into Lexington.
He saw the gilded weathercock
Swim in the moonlight as he passed,
And the meeting-house windows, blank and bare,
Gazed at him with a spectral glare.

It was two by the village clock
When he came to the bridge in Concord town.
He heard the bleating of the flock
And the twitter of birds among the trees
And felt the breath of the morning breeze
Blowing over the meadows brown.

So through the night rode Paul Revere;
And so through the night went his cry of alarm
To every Middlesex village and farm—
A cry of defiance and not of fear,
A voice in the darkness, a knock at the door,
And a word that shall echo forevermore!

For, borne on the night-wind of the Past,
Through all our history, to the last,
In the hour of darkness and peril and need,
The people will waken and listen to hear
The hurrying hoof-beats of that steed
And the midnight message of Paul Revere.

PAUL REVERE

Which Moment

Garnett Ann Schultz

Which moment of the day is best?
    So oft I wonder this
At sunrise as I start my day.
    I feel an angel's kiss,
And certainly my heart delights.
    This is a special time;
I breathe a prayer in quietness
    And call this moment mine.

As shadows fall in afternoon
   Across the greening lawn,
This moment is a treasured one
   With morning hours now gone.
I'm very sure this is the best;
   No other can compare.
I pause within the still of day
   To catch the breeze so fair.

And then the sunset blazes forth
   Within the western sky,
The world so hushed in evening's hour
   As breezes seem to sigh.
I know a peace within my heart
   And think of each bright quest;
Within my mind I'm certain then
   Each moment is the best.

HANDMADE HEIRLOOM

◆ ◆ ◆

FABRIC-COVERED PICTURE FRAME. Crafted by Mary Skarmeas. Jerry Koser Photography.

FABRIC-COVERED PICTURE FRAME

Mary Skarmeas

When I began looking into the craft of fabric-covered picture frames, I was pleasantly reminded of a time many years ago when, as a child of six or seven, I learned from my mother how to make a simple frame for my first school photograph. With some colorful yarn and two squares of cardboard glued one on top of the other to form an eight-point star, we created a frame for my new black and white school portrait—a frame that made the photograph seem worthy of hanging on a wall. Instead of putting my school picture in an album, to be seen only on rare occasions, or in a dresser drawer among dozens of other photos with no place of their own, my picture had a frame, and thus a place of honor on the wall of my mother's bedroom. It was a very special accomplishment for a shy little girl.

Whether of yarn and cardboard or finely carved mahogany, frames confer a special status on the images they encase. They highlight the pictures that touch our hearts, the photos that capture life as we remember it. When placed in the perfect frame, the simplest drawing becomes a work of art and the most haphazard snapshot becomes a moment worth treasuring.

For centuries, artists have understood this ability of a frame to complete and complement the object it surrounds. Before frames were created, artists often painted them directly onto the canvas. Other frames were part of a building's architecture; artists would draw attention to their murals by painting them on a wall that stood between two majestic columns. Or in cathedrals and palaces, doorways were purposefully placed where they would frame a view of the building's interior.

Through the years, frames became works of art in their own right. Craftsmen elaborately carved frames of wood and inlaid them with ebony, mother of pearl, gold, or silver. As new techniques and materials came into vogue, frames evolved and changed to reflect the tastes of the times. Fashions sometimes favored spartan frames with simple designs; other frames were so detailed and ornate that they competed with the paintings they held. During the Victorian era, popular women's magazines began publishing instructions for do-it-yourself frames made from everyday materials. Fabric-covered picture frames began then as women discovered they could make beautiful frames from scraps of material in their sewing baskets.

Handmade frames make a statement; we award only the most treasured photographs and keepsakes such special treatment. Choices include wedding photos, snapshots of family gatherings, a baby's first photo, pressed flowers from a special bouquet, a wedding invitation.

The Victorian era inspired the rich colors and textures of elegant silk moiré, damask, and lace that I chose for my fabric-covered frame. To make your own frame, look in crafts books and magazines for detailed instructions. The front of the frame begins as a heavy cardboard picture frame matte found at a crafts store. To make the back piece of the frame, cut another piece of cardboard to the same size as the matte; do not cut an opening in the back piece. Using the frame front as a template, cut one piece of batting to the exact same size; glue the batting in place onto the frame front. Again using the frame front as a template, cut a piece of fabric ⅝-inch larger on all sides than the matte; neatly fold this extra fabric over the edges and glue behind (cut notches at the corners to make the folds smooth). Then cover the frame's back piece with fabric, again folding the extra fabric over the edges and gluing.

To create a pocket to hold your photograph in place, cut a piece of heavy bond paper approximately ½ inch larger than the photo. Glue the sides and bottom of the bond paper behind the opening in the frame front. The photo will slip between the bond paper and the frame front.

Before gluing the frame's front and back together, you can add decorations to complement the fabric. One glance through your sewing basket should yield plenty of creative ideas—delicate white or ivory lace, buttons and bows, satin ribbons and roses. If you have a photograph in mind for your frame, coordinate the colors of the fabric and accents with those in the picture; you can also draw inspiration from the decor of the room where the photo will be displayed.

When you finish decorating, glue the frame front to the frame back, wrong sides together, along the side and bottom edges. The top edge should be left unglued so that your photograph can slide between the frame's front and back pieces. To make an easel stand, cut out a narrow rectangle from cardboard, cover it with fabric, and glue one end to the frame back. Slip in your photo; then find the perfect spot to display your new keepsake for all to see.

Recently, my six-year-old neighbor Cayce came by for a visit, and I noticed her admiring my new fabric-covered frame. I pulled out my crafts box and showed my young friend how to make a simple frame for her recent school picture. Cayce was so proud of the finished product that she gave the framed photo to her mother, who was touched by the gift. I thought of my own mother and my eight-point, cardboard picture frame of so many years ago. I no longer have that photo, but I remember it vividly, along with the warmth of my mother's love and the pride I felt when she hung my framed photo on the wall. Thrown in a drawer, that photo would have been lost; hung on my mother's wall in my handmade frame, it will be forever remembered. Be sure to choose the photos for your fabric-covered frames with care; for once a photograph is given the special distinction of a handmade frame, it is sure to be cherished for years to come.

Mary Skarmeas lives in Danvers, Massachusetts, and has recently earned her bachelor's degree in English at Suffolk University. Mother of four and grandmother of three, Mary loves all crafts, especially knitting.

Remember When

WHEN ATTICS WERE IN STYLE

from *Love and Laughter*

Marjorie Holmes

What a pity, it seems to me, that in this era of ranch houses, so few children have an attic in which to play.

That "storage space" with a pull-down ladder has been made to substitute for what was once a marvelous boon to both mothers and small fry.

"Oh, go to the attic and play," harried parents used to be able to say to noisy offspring on a rainy day. Or, "Please, may we play in the attic?" the youngsters themselves would beg, as a special treat.

What family room, how-ever efficient, or rumpus room, however gay, can offer the adventure, the enchantment, of the attics of yesteryear?

If possible, I would tack an old-fashioned attic onto every modern house. And the specifi-cations would be:

A door that squeaks a little when a child's hands turn the knob. Stairs that are castle-steep and narrow as canyon walls. A window that looks down from the landing like a dusty, slightly scary glass eye...

A mellow and slightly eerie smell for this world of just-under-the-roof. Stale and stuffy, yes, but mysterious and promising, with the tang of the rough, unpainted lumber that tops the house and is intimate with the sky . . .

Long empty alleys for running and yelling and noisily pounding feet. Dark little cubbies for hiding in. Floors thick enough to muffle the racket. Yet cups and hollows of space to echo the wild fruity music of children's shouts . . .

Secret attic sounds of its own: a squirrel scurrying along the eaves. A tree shaking hands with the shingles. The wind whistling by. And on rainy days the rhythm of drops on the roof, cozy as popping corn.

Many things should, of course, be stored in this attic: Halloween costumes. Easter baskets. Great boxes bulging with bells and tinsel and Christmas trimmings. Flags from the Fourth of July. All the accoutrements of a magical children's calendar that boasts only holidays . . .

And there should be mysterious souvenirs to wonder about: thick, plush photograph albums, fastened with silver clasps. Bundles of ribbon-tied letters. Pressed flowers. Tissue-wrapped locks of hair. A child's own baby clothes . . .

And in this attic too there should be treasures for playing house. Porch furniture. Old bridge lamps. Bedsteads. A grandfather's clock. And for the dressing up, trunks of old hats and evening dresses and fancy shoes . . .

Lucky the child who has such an attic for exploring. Lucky the parents. Every house that really means home should have an attic on top!

Ideals'
Family Recipes

Favorite Recipes from the Ideals Family of Readers

Editor's Note: Please send us your best-loved recipes! Mail a typed copy of the recipe along with your name, address, and phone number to Ideals magazine, ATTN: Recipes, P.O. Box 305300, Nashville, Tennessee 37230. We will pay $10 for each recipe used. Recipes cannot be returned.

DEVILED EGG DELIGHTS

In a large bowl, combine 6 hard-boiled eggs, finely chopped; 1 teaspoon minced onion; 3 bacon strips, fried and crumbled; ½ teaspoon salt; ½ teaspoon pepper; ¼ teaspoon prepared mustard; and ¼ cup mayonnaise. Stir until creamy. Form into 1-inch balls. Roll balls in 1 cup finely shredded Cheddar cheese. Cover; refrigerate until serving. Makes 27 balls.

Naomi Dyer
Eaton, Colorado

FAVORITE HOT ROLLS

In a medium bowl, dissolve 1 package dry yeast in ¼ cup warm water. Stir in ½ cup granulated sugar, 2 beaten eggs, 1 cup warm water, ½ cup vegetable oil, 1 teaspoon salt, and 4 cups unsifted, all-purpose flour. Mix well. Cover and refrigerate for 8 hours or overnight. On a floured surface, knead in small amounts of flour until the dough loses its stickiness. Divide dough into 3 parts; roll out each part into a 9-inch circle. Cut each circle into 8 wedges. Starting with the wide edge and rolling toward the point, roll up each section. Place on a greased baking sheet. Cover with a clean cloth, set in a warm place, and let rise 4 hours or until doubled in bulk. Preheat oven to 350° F. Bake 10 to 12 minutes. Makes 24 rolls.

Dorothy Johnson
Greenville, Michigan

FRUIT SALAD

In a large bowl, combine one 3½-ounce package instant vanilla dry pudding mix; one 17-ounce can fruit cocktail in heavy syrup (including syrup); one 20-ounce can pineapple chunks, drained; one 10-ounce jar Maraschino cherries, drained; one 11-ounce can Mandarin oranges, drained; and one 16-ounce can sliced pears, drained. Mix well; chill. Makes 10 servings.

Phyllis M. Peters
Three Rivers, Michigan

BROCCOLI-RICE CASSEROLE

Prepare 2½ cups cooked rice according to package directions; set aside. Cook one 10-ounce package frozen, chopped broccoli according to package directions; drain well and set aside. Preheat oven to 350° F. In a medium skillet, sauté ½ cup chopped celery and ¼ cup chopped onion in 2 tablespoons butter or margarine until tender but not brown.

In a large bowl, combine 1 can condensed cream of mushroom soup, ½ cup milk, and one 8-ounce jar pasteurized process American cheese spread; mix well. Stir in rice, broccoli, and vegetables. Spoon mixture into a 2-quart casserole. Bake 40 to 45 minutes or until thoroughly heated. Makes 6 to 8 servings.

Mrs. Shirley Brennan
Williamsburg, Virginia

HONEY-GLAZED CHICKEN

Preheat oven to 350° F. Cut up 1 frying chicken and place in a plastic bag with 1 cup flour, 1 teaspoon salt, and ¼ teaspoon pepper. Shake to coat chicken evenly. In a 12-inch skillet, heat 1 tablespoon vegetable oil over medium heat. Add chicken and fry 10 to 15 minutes until brown, turning to brown all sides. Transfer chicken to a greased, 9-by-13-inch baking dish.

In a small bowl, combine ½ cup melted butter or margarine, ½ cup honey, and ¼ cup lemon juice. Mix well and pour over chicken; cover with aluminum foil. Bake 45 minutes or until done, basting occasionally. Makes 6 servings.

Linda L. Sanford
Sigourney, Iowa

Simple Splendor

Marcia Krugh Leaser

I found a spot of sunshine
　Hidden in my own backyard.
I barely even noticed,
　For I wasn't looking hard.
But suddenly it caught my eye,
　This brilliant, little stream;
And I could not ignore the glow
　It gave to grasses green
Or how the lazy tulip
　Lifted high its ruby head
To drink in all the splendor
　Of this warming, yellow thread.
Just a tiny bit of sunshine,
　But how it blessed my day,
Bringing joy and gladness
　With its single, golden ray.

Collector's Corner

BIBLES

by Michelle Prater Burke

On a low shelf near my favorite reading chair stands a row of Bibles, wedged together in no particular order, from a stout, new version with an uncreased cover to a small book of Psalms whose spine long ago lost its title.

When I need an inspiring word, I reach for one of the volumes, often deciding on my grandfather's faded King James Version, which I keep within arm's reach of my chair. Instantly, I'm reminded of childhood visits to my grandparents' farm, where Granddaddy could often be found reading from the family Bible, its cracked leather cover fitting comfortably in his hands. He held the book as if it were an old friend to be respected; and to the grandchildren that gathered around him, he made the stories come alive.

Perhaps these memories naturally led me to begin my own collection of Bibles, which now includes several volumes. One of my favorite pieces is a weighty family Bible I discovered at an estate sale. A gold ribbon marks the page where, in 1910, a young mother named Elizabeth began to record the events in her family's life, from births to baptisms to weddings to deaths. I never knew Elizabeth or her relatives who fill the old Bible's family tree; yet I feel an unexplained connection to her, a shared importance of family, of values, of God.

COVER SHEET TO A GERMAN TRANSLATION OF THE BIBLE, 1706.
Archive for Art and History, Berlin. Superstock.

Several Bibles in my collection retell my *own* life story; there is the children's Bible with the zippered, white leather cover that I renewed with white shoe polish each spring; the small New Testament that I earned at Sunday School when I first recited all sixty-six books of the Bible; the black leather, gold-engraved Bible my parents gave me when I left home after graduation.

Through the years, I've added many old, collectible editions that offer interesting commentaries, typographic devices, or illustrations. At a recent antiquarian book sale, I purchased a nineteenth-century American Bible full of ornate illuminations, a great find for any collector. As I slid my latest purchase among my other Bibles, I momentarily considered placing my new treasure in the coveted spot beside my reading chair. I changed my mind as I glanced at the cover of Granddaddy's Bible; for with that ragged cover come grand memories of hearing parables at my grandfather's knee.

Undoubtedly, every old Bible in my collection has its own unique history; whether it was held during a wedding ceremony or carried in a soldier's chest pocket, each has shared the life of its readers. Examining my collection, I notice the creased spines, wrinkled pages, and scribbled margins—timeworn marks left by previous owners and myself alike. The marks I've made on these Bibles, however, could never compare to the invisible marks they've left on me.

BIBLE COLLECTING FACTS

If you would like to start a collection of Bibles, here are some tips to help you get started:

HISTORY
• In 1382, John Wycliffe completed the first English translation of the entire Bible. Two hundred of these hand-written manuscripts still exist.
• The first book every printed was a Latin Bible printed in approximately 1455 in Germany by Johann Gutenberg. Forty-eight original Gutenberg Bibles still exist.
• In 1526, William Tyndale's translation was the first printed New Testament in English.
• Miles Coverdale edited the first printed English translation of the entire Bible in 1535.
• In 1604, James the First of England ordered a new English translation. The King James Version was first published in 1611.
• Published in Philadelphia in 1782, the Aitken Bible was the first English Bible printed in the United States.
• Bibles were often sold by subscription. Buyers would purchase a few leaves at a time; when a numbered set was complete, they would choose their own binder and artist.

FOCUSING COLLECTIONS
Since literally millions of Bibles have been printed, collectors often choose to focus their collections on one particular kind of Bible. Some examples include:
• Bibles from a specific time period or published in a certain geographical area
• First editions of notable versions of the Bible, such as the first complete Bible translated by a woman: the Julia E. Smith Bible of 1876
• Bibles once owned by notable people or Bible scholars

SWEDISH BIBLE. Marshall Prescott, Unicorn Stock Photos.

• Bibles translated into different languages
• Beautifully produced volumes that offer fine type, illustrations, and binding
• Bibles with title pages that credit distinctive private presses
• Various modern translations, such as the Revised Standard Version or the New International Version.

INTERESTING EXAMPLES
• Rare, valuable, handwritten manuscripts dated before 1455
• Bibles with covers flaunting needlework, semi-precious stones, or metal bindings
• Bibles with interior woodcuts, engravings, or colorful artwork
• Miniature Bibles, only four inches high or smaller
• A child's "rebus paraphrase" Bible that substituted pictures in place of many words, published in Connecticut in 1830
• "Nickname" Bibles that have acquired humorous monikers due to misprints in text
• Pocket-sized Gospels printed for Civil War soldiers

Redbird on a Dogwood Tree

Mary Jeannette Bassett

Redbird on a dogwood tree,
Pour out your soul in melody!
Let me hear each thrilling note
As it leaves your quivering throat,
Make me feel that every vein
Pulses with your spring refrain,
Melt my heart with warmth anew,
Gladden me the whole day through.
If I find my task too long,
Cheer me with your joyous song.
Redbird on a dogwood tree,
Let me share your ecstasy!

A Choir of Joy

Ave Maria Plover

As daylight fast approaches
And nature starts to stir,
An early morn recital
From the robins can be heard.

They lift their voices merrily
While sweet sounds cross the skies.
Their lovely music fills my room
And greets me as I rise.

With heads held back in harmony,
They sing out loud and strong.
God's creatures sit attentively
To hear each happy song.

There is no chorus on the earth
More precious to my heart
Or one that brings more joy and peace
To each new day I start.

For a bird of the air shall
carry the voice, and that which
hath wings shall tell the matter.

Ecclesiastes 10:20

Devotions FROM THE Heart

Pamela Kennedy

Blessed be the God and Father of our Lord Jesus Christ, which according to his abundant mercy hath begotten us again unto a lively hope by the resurrection of Jesus Christ from the dead.

–I Peter 1:3

THE RESURRECTION OF DREAMS

I have always been a planner. As a child I organized my dolls and planned their daily activities. In school I thrived in a classroom with an organized teacher and felt adrift when assigned to a less-structured, spontaneous sort. Lists and schedules became my security—a way to control and direct the uncertainties of life, a way to realize my dreams.

As a young wife I took pride in maintaining an orderly home. Grocery shopping was done on a budget and with a list. Housework was organized by each day. Work came before play and duty before relaxation. With an orderly approach, life was manageable. I knew my dreams could be achieved with the appropriate amount of organization and hard work.

And then we decided to have a family. According to my timeline, it was time to begin to have babies one year after marriage. One year passed, then two, then three, and no babies arrived. The structure of my life started to crumble. Frantic to regain control, I became more organized—reading, studying, seeking guidance from experts in infertility.

Three years turned to five and still no babies came. Slowly I began to accept the death of my dream; my dream of a house full of laughing children, of walks in the park and noisy family holidays. Year by year, tear by tear, the dream faded. It could not be bought with all the power of my will, nor all the planning of my heart.

Then a new hope flickered. We began to explore adoption. But circumstances conspired against us: there were few babies available, the waiting time was more than two years, and my husband was due to be transferred within eighteen months. Appointments with social workers were delayed or canceled.

Then the impossible happened. On a sunny June day, four weeks before we were to move, we walked out of the adoption center carrying our seven-week-old son. No amount of planning, preparing, or maneuvering had brought about this miracle. It was simply an act of God's mercy. It was the resurrection of hope from a dead dream.

So often we experience the loss of hope when our dreams die. Perhaps a relationship fails, a promise is broken, a child disappoints. We plunge into the tomb-like darkness of despair, certain that life will never be bright again. It is at this point, however, that God often works His greatest miracle. It is the miracle of the resurrection. He is not limited by the death of our dreams but enabled by it. For when our hands are emptied of our own plans, He is able to fill them with His abundance.

That first Easter morning, Mary, Peter, John, and the others believed their dreams were dead, trapped in a stony crypt. What God revealed, however, was a new dream far more wonderful than they could have imagined. Where they saw death, He had prepared new life and a dream that changed the course of history.

When you believe your dreams have died, look upon the empty tomb. In His loving mercy, God has a new dream waiting for you, a lively hope made possible because of the resurrection of His Son.

Dear Father, When I am disappointed and discouraged, help me remember
that You have prepared a new dream for me. Guide me to experience
the resurrection power available because of Your mercy.
AMEN.

Nest Eggs

Robert Louis Stevenson

Birds all the sunny day
　　Flutter and quarrel
Here in the arbour-like
　　Tent of the laurel.

Here in the fork
　　The brown nest is seated;
Four little blue eggs
　　The mother keeps heated.

While we stand watching her,
　　Staring like gabies
Safe in each egg are the
　　Bird's little babies.

Soon the frail eggs they shall
　　Chip, and upspringing
Make all the April woods
　　Merry with singing.

Younger than we are,
　　O children, and frailer,
Soon in blue air they'll be,
　　Singer and sailor.

We, so much older,
　　Taller and stronger,
We shall look down on the
　　Birdies no longer.

They shall go flying
　　With musical speeches
High overhead in the
　　Tops of the beeches.

In spite of our wisdom
　　And sensible talking,
We on our feet must go
　　Plodding and walking.

Spring's Recurring Magic

May Smith White

Some days are set apart
   from all the rest,
And even birds seem
   reverent to these;
Each mute in song,
   each on her new-made nest—
Time hesitates—
   no hurried moment flees.

I yearn to hold such days
   close to my heart
That I may somehow feel
   each one is mine;
Then faith will form
   the underlying part

As Spring weaves true
   her intricate design.

But much too soon
   this beauty will be lost,
The quietness gone
   that I have often felt;
And summer's burning sun
   will sear, like frost,
Soft greening carpets
   where my heart has knelt.
Yet each recurring Spring
   calls forth some power
To claim her sacred charm
   with every hour.

The first day of the week cometh Mary Magdalene early, when it was yet dark, unto the sepulchre . . . . Jesus saith unto her, "Mary." . . .

—John 20:1, 16

First Appearance

Sara Henderson Hay

In all His resurrected grace,
How easily He might have come
And, meeting Pilate face to face,
Stricken him dumb.

How well this Jesus might have stood
Suddenly in the city square
And watched the stricken multitude
Tremble and stare.

With what immensity of right
He could have come again and thrust
The council into outer night,
The law to dust.

How like the gentle Mary's Son
To put aside the whirlwind reaping
And minister to the need of one
Who sought Him, weeping.

How blessed beyond the proudest word
Was Mary Magdalene, who came
Early unto the tomb and heard
Christ speak her name!

The Entry

And when they drew nigh unto Jerusalem, and were come to Bethphage, unto the mount of Olives, then sent Jesus two disciples, Saying unto them, Go into the village over against you, and straightway ye shall find an ass tied, and a colt with her: loose them, and bring them unto me. And if any man say ought unto you, ye shall say, The Lord hath need of them; and straightway he will send them.

All this was done, that it might be fulfilled which was spoken by the prophet, saying, Tell ye the daughter of Sion, Behold, thy King cometh unto thee, meek, and sitting upon an ass, and a colt the foal of an ass. And the disciples went, and did as Jesus commanded them, And brought the ass, and the colt, and put on them their clothes, and they set him thereon. And a very great multitude spread their garments in the way; others cut down branches from the trees, and strawed them in the way.

And the multitudes that went before, and that followed, cried, saying, Hosanna to the son of David: Blessed is he that cometh in the name of the Lord; Hosanna in the highest. And when he was come into Jerusalem, all the city was moved, saying, Who is this? And the multitude said, This is Jesus the prophet of Nazareth of Galilee.

MATTHEW 21:1-11

The Last Supper

And the first day of unleavened bread, when they killed the passover, his disciples said unto him, Where wilt thou that we go and prepare that thou mayest eat the passover?

And he sendeth forth two of his disciples, and saith unto them, Go ye into the city, and there shall meet you a man bearing a pitcher of water: follow him. And wheresoever he shall go in, say ye to the goodman of the house, The Master saith, Where is the guestchamber, where I shall eat the passover with my disciples? And he will shew you a large upper room furnished and prepared: there make ready for us.

And his disciples went forth, and came into the city, and found as he had said unto them: and they made ready the passover. And in the evening he cometh with the twelve. And as they did eat, Jesus took bread, and blessed, and brake it, and gave to them, and said, Take, eat: this is my body. And he took the cup, and when he had given thanks, he gave it to them: and they all drank of it.

And he said unto them, This is my blood of the new testament, which is shed for many. Verily I say unto you, I will drink no more of the fruit of the vine, until that day that I drink it new in the kingdom of God.

MARK 14:12-17, 22-25

Walk to Calvary

When the morning was come, all the chief priests and elders of the people took counsel against Jesus to put him to death: And when they had bound him, they led him away, and delivered him to Pontius Pilate the governor.

And Jesus stood before the governor: and the governor asked him, saying, Art thou the King of the Jews? And Jesus said unto him, Thou sayest. And when he was accused of the chief priests and elders, he answered nothing. Then said Pilate unto him, Hearest thou not how many things they witness against thee? And he answered him to never a word; insomuch that the governor marvelled greatly.

Now at that feast the governor was wont to release unto the people a prisoner, whom they would. And they had then a notable prisoner, called Barabbas. Therefore when they were gathered together, Pilate said unto them, Whom will ye that I release unto you? Barabbas, or Jesus which is called Christ? For he knew that for envy they had delivered him. The governor answered and said unto them, Whether of the twain will ye that I release unto you? They said, Barabbas. Pilate saith unto them, What shall I do then with Jesus which is called Christ? They all say unto him, Let him be crucified.

Then the soldiers of the governor took Jesus into the common hall, and gathered unto him the whole band of soldiers. And they stripped him, and put on him a scarlet robe. And after that they had mocked him, they took the robe off from him, and put his own raiment on him, and led him away to crucify him.

MATTHEW 27:1, 2, 11-18, 21-22, 27-28, 31

The Crucifixion

And Pilate answered and said again unto them, What will ye then that I shall do unto him whom ye call the King of the Jews? And they cried out again, Crucify him. Then Pilate said unto them, Why, what evil hath he done? And they cried out the more exceedingly, Crucify him.

And so Pilate, willing to content the people, released Barabbas unto them, and delivered Jesus, when he had scourged him, to be crucified. And the soldiers led him away into the hall, called Praetorium; and they call together the whole band. And they clothed him with purple, and platted a crown of thorns, and put it about his head, And began to salute him, Hail, King of the Jews! And they smote him on the head with a reed, and did spit upon him, and bowing their knees worshipped him. And when they had mocked him, they took off the purple from him, and put his own clothes on him, and led him out to crucify him.

And it was the third hour, and they crucified him.

MARK 15:12-20, 25

The Deposition

And Jesus cried with a loud voice, and gave up the ghost. And the veil of the temple was rent in twain from the top to the bottom. And when the centurion, which stood over against him, saw that he so cried out, and gave up the ghost, he said, Truly this man was the Son of God.

There were also women looking on afar off: among whom was Mary Magdalene, and Mary the mother of James the less and of Joses, and Salome; And now when the even was come, because it was the preparation, that is, the day before the sabbath, Joseph of Arimathaea, an honourable counsellor, which also waited for the kingdom of God, came, and went in boldly unto Pilate, and craved the body of Jesus.

And Pilate marvelled if he were already dead: and calling unto him the centurion, he asked him whether he had been any while dead. And when he knew it of the centurion, he gave the body to Joseph. And he bought fine linen, and took him down, and wrapped him in the linen, and laid him in a sepulchre which was hewn out of a rock, and rolled a stone unto the door of the sepulchre.

MARK 15:37-40, 42-46

The Resurrection

But Mary stood without at the sepulchre weeping: and as she wept, she stooped down, and looked into the sepulchre, And seeth two angels in white sitting, the one at the head, and the other at the feet, where the body of Jesus had lain. And they say unto her, Woman, why weepest thou? She saith unto them, Because they have taken away my Lord, and I know not where they have laid him.

And when she had thus said, she turned herself back, and saw Jesus standing, and knew not that it was Jesus. Jesus saith unto her, Woman, why weepest thou? whom seekest thou? She, supposing him to be the gardener, saith unto him, Sir, if thou have borne him hence, tell me where thou hast laid him, and I will take him away.

Jesus saith unto her, Mary. She turned herself, and saith unto him, Rabboni; which is to say, Master. Jesus saith unto her, Touch me not; for I am not yet ascended to my Father: but go to my brethren, and say unto them, I ascend unto my Father, and your Father; and to my God, and your God.

JOHN 20:11-17

The Ascension

And he said unto them, These are the words which I spake unto you, while I was yet with you, that all things must be fulfilled, which were written in the law of Moses, and in the prophets, and in the psalms, concerning me.

Then opened he their understanding, that they might understand the scriptures, And said unto them, Thus it is written, and thus it behoved Christ to suffer, and to rise from the dead the third day: And ye are witnesses of these things.

And he led them out as far as to Bethany, and he lifted up his hands, and blessed them. And it came to pass, while he blessed them, he was parted from them, and carried up into heaven.

And they worshipped him, and returned to Jerusalem with great joy: And were continually in the temple, praising and blessing God. Amen.

LUKE 24:44-46, 48, 50-53

ASCENSION
Tres Riches Heures du Duc de Berry
Limbourg Brothers
Musée Conde, Chantilly, France
Giraudon/Art Resource, New York

THROUGH MY WINDOW

Pamela Kennedy

Art by Ron Adair

SIMON PETER, THE ROCK

Peter leaned toward the fire, extending his hands against the heat. His palms burned, but the chill of foreboding and dread, the icy pain of self-doubt and blame still filled his chest. So much had happened in just a few hours. He recalled the warmth of fellowship in the upper room and how it had been shattered by Jesus' announcement that He would soon be betrayed. When Peter protested, declaring his devotion, the Master only shook His head sadly and predicted that even Peter would disown Him three times before the cock crowed. The shame of those words still stung.

Later, in Gethsemane, Peter was unable even to stay awake while Jesus prayed. His heart ached under the gentle rebuke of the one he loved and served. And then when Judas led the angry mob to arrest Jesus, Peter tried to defend his Master, lop-ping off the ear of Malchus, servant to the high priest. Jesus' touch healed the servant's ear, but His words wounded the impulsive disciple once again: "Put your sword away! Shall I not drink the cup the Father has given me?"

Now, in the courtyard of the high priest, Peter shivered near the fire. Somewhere inside the walls Jesus was being questioned, perhaps even beaten, and here in fear and shame sat the disciple who had vowed to follow Him even to death. Jesus once called him Peter, the rock. He had once walked on water, even cast out demons and healed the sick through the power of God. Now he longed only to hide within the shadows.

"Aren't you one of His disciples?"

Peter, startled from his thoughts, looked up at the servant girl quickly. "No!" he replied, "you must be mistaken."

She studied him a moment, then moved on. Peter felt sweat break out on his forehead. He noted the glances of the others near the fire and shifted his position in an effort to appear unconcerned.

"Didn't I see you in the garden at the time of the man's arrest?"

Peter's heart pounded in his ears, and he raised his voice to drown it out. "No! I tell you I don't know the man!" He rose in anger and stalked across the courtyard to the gate.

The others, like hunters cornering their prey, followed him. One approached with a malevolent and triumphant expression and announced to the others, "You can tell by his Galilean accent that he's one of them."

In a desperate fury, Peter shook his fist and swore, "I don't even know who you are talking about!"

His fist was still in the air when a rooster's crow echoed in the courtyard. The sound pierced Peter's heart as the words of Christ raced through his mind: "Before the cock crows you will disown me three times." Blindly, he fumbled with the iron gate, stumbling into the darkness beyond.

Like a man possessed, Peter ran through the dark streets of Jerusalem, his breath coming in sobs. Reaching the house where the disciples had taken the Passover, he dashed up the stone stairway to the upper room, pushed open the heavy wooden door, entered and bolted it behind him. In the dimness he saw the alarm on the faces of several of the other disciples. Peter collapsed in the corner of the room hiding his face in his hands.

For two days and nights the frightened disciples cowered in the upper room. They clung to each other when the earth shook at midday and listened in awe as John returned from the crucifixion to relate the scene and recount their Lord's last words. No one dared to leave; their meals were eaten in solemn silence, each one lost in his own thoughts and fears.

On the morning of the first day of the week, shortly after dawn, there was a pounding at the door. Carefully, Peter opened it a crack. Mary of Magdala pushed past him, her face alight with wonder, her breath coming in rapid bursts.

"I have seen the Lord!" she announced. "He is alive. He has risen from the dead!" She wheeled around and pointed at the dumfounded fishermen. "And there was an angel who said you should all go to Galilee because Jesus would meet you there!" Mary's eyes blazed with an unearthly fervor, and

tendrils of dark hair clung to her flushed cheeks.

One of the men leaned toward her and whispered, "You are mad, woman. Your grief has overcome you. The Master is dead. John saw it all at Golgotha."

"No, no! You don't understand. He was dead, but now he's not!" She looked imploringly at the incredulous men. "The tomb is empty, I tell you. Our Lord lives!"

Mary dashed past Peter and disappeared down the stairway in a rush of flapping robes as she hastily threw her veil over her hair.

Peter stared at the open door, Mary's words echoing in his mind: The tomb empty? The Lord alive?

Suddenly, John ran through the doorway and Peter's indecision dissipated. He followed after the other disciple, trailing him through the streets until they reached the tomb. John stopped at the opening, staring into the darkness within; but Peter, impelled by his unreasonable hope, dashed into the sepulchre and then froze, gaping at the scene before him. On the stony bier lay the linen bindings that Joseph and Nicodemus had lovingly wrapped around Jesus' body only a few days earlier. The wrappings were undisturbed, still wound as if around a form, but empty and limp. It was as if the body had evaporated, leaving the burial cloths like an empty shell.

Peter was aware of movement behind him and turned to see John approaching the bier. John's face registered incredulity at first and then a light of understanding began to dawn. The men looked at one another, then John gripped Peter's arm.

"It's true!" he whispered.

Peter nodded slowly, his mind racing to grasp what his heart was already beginning to accept. If the Lord is alive, there is hope—hope for forgiveness, for restoration, for healing. If the Lord is alive, Peter could be freed from his prison of regret and guilt; freed to be the rock that Jesus had once challenged him to become. Peter had entered that room of death a broken, empty man, but he would leave it whole and filled. If Jesus is alive, nothing is impossible.

Pamela Kennedy is a freelance writer of short stories, articles, essays, and children's books. Wife of a naval officer and mother of three children, she has made her home on both U.S. coasts and currently resides in Honolulu, Hawaii. She draws her material from her own experiences and memories, adding highlights from her imagination to enhance the story.

The Christ
of Easter

J. Harold Gwynne

We praise the Christ of Easter
Who tore the bars away
In resurrection power
And rose on Easter Day.

No other shares His glory
As risen Lord of life;
No other name can conquer
The world and all its strife.

The risen Lord assures us
Of life beyond the grave;
His gift is life eternal;
For us His life He gave.

All hail the Christ of Easter,
The everlasting Thou!
Before Him all shall worship,
And every knee shall bow.

My Saviour Lives

Kay Hoffman

I was not in the garden
In the early morning gloom
When the women came with spices
And found the empty tomb.

I did not see the risen Lord
Walk in the garden fair
Or hear Him speak with gentle voice
To Mary weeping there.

But I have seen a lily bloom
From sod yet cold and bleak,
And in the cooing of a dove
I hear His voice so sweet.

I was not in the garden,
And I did not play a part.
Yet still, I know my Saviour lives;
He lives within my heart.

Sweet Easter Hope

Kay Hoffman

The darkened tomb is empty now;
Gone is the deep despair.
The risen Lord on garden path
Gives hope beyond compare.

In Christ we have forgiveness;
With His blood He bought our sins.
In Him there's Easter promise;
He arose to live again.

He is the way, the truth, the life;
Through faith in Him we come
To enter in through heaven's gate
When this life's work is done.

Because Christ died and now He lives
Our hearts rejoice today!
No longer need we fear the tomb;
The stone is rolled away.

AGAVE ON FIRST OUTLOOK
Ansel Adams
Sweeney/Rubin Ansel Adams Fiat Lux Collection
UCR/California Museum of Photography
University of California, Riverside

Rainy Morning

M. H. Watkins

When lightly ebbs the silent rain
    And day dawns dark upon the hills,
The grasses droop their sodden heads
    And softly weep the daffodils.

I mount the rock which stands afar
    To gaze upon the drizzled land
And touch the leafy boughs of trees,
    Which leave their tears upon my hand.

The misty morn is solemn, still;
    For gentle falls the silent dew.
And cool the dawn so wrapped in gray,
    Which softens every brilliant hue.

The quiet moment brings its peace
    And gives new strength to make me whole.
I lift my face to feel the rain
    Which cleanses body, heart, and soul.

RAINDROPS ON HAREBELLS
Rockport, Maine
William Johnson
Johnson's Photography

Lisa C. Ragan

Ansel Adams

Throughout the twentieth century, the conservation movement in the United States grew steadily as Americans began to realize the precarious state of their wilderness areas. National parks became a priority to the American people for the first time; and as the idea of preserving the land gained popularity, the great American photographer Ansel Adams used his talents to promote the cause of the conservation movement. Throughout his life, Adams successfully combined his love of nature with the fine art of his photography to produce some of the most influential images in the history of photography.

I constantly return to the elements of nature that surrounded me in my childhood, to both the vision and the mood. —*Ansel Adams*

Ansel Adams was born on February 20, 1902, in San Francisco, to Olive Bray Adams and Charles Hitchcock Adams. Situated on a stretch of dunes beyond the Golden Gate, the family home was a quiet place where Adams grew up exploring every rocky outcropping and sea creature he could find. The rugged terrain near his home was his playground, and those early days closely connected with the natural world had a profound impact on Adams that directed the course of his life's work.

I knew my destiny when I first experienced Yosemite.

At age fourteen, Adams's Aunt Mary gave him a copy of *In the Heart of the Sierras* by J. M. Hutchings to read while he was in bed with a cold. Adams devoured every word and convinced his parents that the family must visit this mysterious wonderland. In June of 1916, Adams first visited Yosemite: "We finally emerged at Valley View—the splendor of Yosemite burst upon us and it *was* glorious. . . . One wonder after another descended upon us; I recall not only the colossal but the little things: the grasses and ferns, cool atriums of the forests." Adams returned to Yosemite every summer for the rest of his life; it became for him a source of spiritual renewal that provided inspiration and deep joy.

I do not know any photographer who was not thrilled over his first exposures and who does not continue to be excited as his pictures evolve and his craft improves.

That first trip to Yosemite at age fourteen was significant for many reasons. In addition to intensifying his love for the natural world, Yosemite was the place where Adams's parents gave him his first Kodak Box Brownie camera. Even though Adams was intrigued with the camera and its possibilities, he considered it only a hobby. Gradually, Adams embraced photography as his life's work. As his spectacular photographs gained notoriety and critical acclaim, Adams became well-known for his technical innovations in photography and published several texts, including *Making a Photograph: An Introduction to Photography*.

Photography is an investigation of both the outer and the inner worlds.

As Adams matured as a photographer and developed his art, he looked inside himself to discover his own personal photographic direction. He detested the popular photographic style of the 1930s, which was mostly soft, pictorial images in the style of the Impressionistic painters. Instead, Adams was drawn to the straightforward, realistic style that a few young photographers were using. Adams sought to combine this form of photography with his wonder of nature. Even when his peers criticized him for shooting subjects of seemingly little social value, Adams continued to concentrate on his wilderness subjects and disappeared into Yosemite whenever possible. Ironically, his images eventually had a profound social impact as important symbols of the conservation movement in America.

I believe in beauty. I believe in stones and water, air and soil, people and their future and their fate.

Adams honed his photographic style in Yosemite, and it was there that he became acquainted with the Sierra Club, a conservation organization founded by John Muir in 1892. Adams joined their ranks at age eighteen and later served on the board of directors for thirty-seven years. Drawn to the Sierra Club's aims to preserve America's natural resources for future generations, Adams worked to promote their aims throughout his life.

People are surprised when I say that I never intentionally made a creative photograph that related directly to an environmental issue. . . .

Adams took his personal vision of America's natural beauty with him to Washington, D.C., where, on numerous occasions, he lobbied Congress on behalf of the Sierra Club. In the mid-1930s, Adams's photography impressed Secretary of the Interior Harold Ickes, who later hired Adams to photograph reclamation projects, Indian reservations, and national parks. It was Ickes who helped Adams in his efforts for the Sierra Club to see Kings Canyon National Park established, a feat achieved in 1940. Perhaps the culmination of Adams's work in Washington came in 1980, when President Jimmy Carter awarded him the Presidential Medal of Freedom in recognition of his conservation efforts for America.

I go out into the world and hope I will come across something that imperatively interests me. I am addicted to the found object. I have no doubt that I will continue to make photographs till my last breath.

Ansel Adams died on the evening of Easter Sunday in 1984. A master of photography and champion of America's wilderness, Adams valued the beauty of nature as a kind of spiritual oasis, a retreat from modern life. His dream was that the splendors of nature in America be preserved and protected for future generations, and the single-minded determination he employed in his art of photography helped to place a clear image of that dream in the minds of the American people.

A Garden

Isla Paschal Richardson

A garden is a place
    wherein to cleanse
The soul of petty thoughts.
    Where flowers nod,
To let the dew refresh
    our wilting dreams,
A place wherein to find ourselves—
    and God.

Spring Parade

Nora M. Bozeman

I love to watch a storm-filled sky
　　As thunderheads erupt on high
And lightning zigzags interplay
　　Like bright Fourth-of-July displays.

I love to watch warm April rain
　　Cascading down my windowpane;
And when the gray clouds disappear,
　　They leave a rainbow souvenir.

I love to watch the sun at play
　　As saucy clouds salute the day
And bluebirds sweetly serenade
　　Their welcome to the spring parade.

SAN CARLOS BORROMEO DEL RIO CARMELO
Carmel, California

Gazing upon the grand mission of San Carlos Borromeo del Rio Carmelo, I find it nearly impossible to imagine that the poet Robert Louis Stevenson, laying eyes upon the church in the 1870s, saw only ruin and disrepair. "When the Carmel church is in the dust, not all the wealth of the states and territories can replace what has been lost," Stevenson wrote of the then more than one-hundred-year-old mission in a book of his travels across the American west. The poet was wise in recognizing the mission's unique beauty and historic value; and thanks in part to his concern, the San Carlos Borromeo I discovered today is a sparkling gem, restored to its original beauty to serve tourists as a museum of California's rich history.

Located in the city of Carmel, on California's Monterey peninsula, San Carlos Borromeo was part of the Spanish attempt to bring Christianity to the native peoples of California and establish Spain's claim to land in the Southwest. Between 1769 and 1823, Franciscan missionaries, with the help of Mexican stonemasons and Native American labor, built a string of more than twenty missions along *El Camino Real,* the "Royal Road" that runs along the California coastline. As civilian towns grew up around the missions, the churches became the backbone of the social, agricultural, and industrial life of Spanish California, only to be abandoned and forgotten when Spain lost its hold in the New World. The missions held on, silent and patient, until the 1930s, when Californians realized they must act or lose part of their history forever.

Restoration of San Carlos Borromeo, commonly known as Mission Carmel, began in 1931. The process took fifty years, but visitors can now enjoy the mission's original, spectacular architecture. An unknown, professional stonemason from Mexico most likely designed the church; his high aspirations, combined with the efforts of unskilled labor, resulted in an amazing architectural creation. As I approached the mission, the sandstone, mined from local hills, glistened in the spring sunshine. I was awed by the church's most distinctive feature, a grand Moorish-style tower crowned with an egg-shaped dome and catenary arches (the only stone ceiling arches in any California mission). Immersed in the serenity of the place, I strolled through the quiet garden until a window on the tower caught my eye, an absolutely brilliant window in the shape of a four-pointed star that tilted slightly to the right above the church's door. The window seemed almost out of place, an ornate focal point on a facade of smooth and simple lines. Once inside, however, I discovered what the window foretold— a breathtakingly lavish interior of reds and golds and painted decorations.

Near the church's sanctuary lies the grave of Junipero Serra, the Spanish priest who led the mission movement. Standing in the silent church, I wondered what Serra and the poet Stevenson would think of how San Carlos Borromeo del Rio Carmelo has risen from the years of neglect. Stevenson lamented that the mission, a monument to California's history of Spanish influence, had fallen into disrepair. Today, just as the window on the facade draws the visitor into the marvelous interior of the church, this wonderfully restored mission draws travelers to Carmel, where a page from California's history is written in the sandstone.

A SLICE OF LIFE

— Edgar A. Guest —

THE LITTLE CHURCH

The little church of long ago,
    Where as a boy I sat
With mother in the family pew,
    And fumbled with my hat—
How I would like to see it now
    The way I saw it then,
The straight-backed pews, the pulpit high,
    The women and the men
Dressed stiffly in their Sunday clothes
    And solemnly devout,
Who closed their eyes when prayers were said
    And never looked about.
That little church of long ago,
    It wasn't grand to see;
But even as a little boy
    It meant a lot to me.

The choir loft where Father sang
    Comes back to me again.
I hear his tenor voice once more
    The way I heard it when
The deacons used to pass the plate;
    And once again I see
The people fumbling for their coins,
    As glad as they could be
To drop their quarters on the plate,
    And I'm a boy once more
With my two pennies in my fist
    That Mother gave before
We left the house; and once again
    I'm reaching out to try
To drop them on the plate before
    The deacon passes by.

It seems to me I'm sitting in
    That high-backed pew, the while
The minister is preaching in
    That good old-fashioned style;
And though I couldn't understand it all
    Somehow I know
The Bible was the text book
    In that church of long ago.
He didn't preach on politics,
    But used the word of God;
And even now I seem to see
    The people gravely nod,
As though agreeing thoroughly
    With all he had to say,
And then I see them thanking him
    Before they go away.

The little church of long ago
    Was not a structure huge;
It had no hired singers
    Or no other subterfuge
To get the people to attend.
    'Twas just a simple place
Where every Sunday we were told
    About God's saving grace.
No men of wealth were gathered there
    To help it with a gift;
The only worldly thing it had—
    A mortgage hard to lift.
And somehow, dreaming here today,
    I wish that I could know
The joy of once more sitting
    In that church of long ago.

Edgar A. Guest began his illustrious career in 1895 at the age of fourteen when his work first appeared in the Detroit Free Press. His column was syndicated in over three hundred newspapers, and he became known as "The Poet of the People."

Garden Magic

Edna Jaques

She has the gift of growing things,
The magic touch with plant and flower;
The frailest slips will grow for her,
Touched by her finger's tender power.
We asked her how she made them grow;
She laughed and said she loved them so.

Her windowsills are always bright
With blooms of every shade and hue;
She's always setting out new bulbs,
You know the way some women do.
She digs around the soil and sands,
Patting it down with loving hands.

And sometimes just when twilight creeps
Across the gardens of the town,
I see her walking lovingly
Amongst her flowers up and down,
Her garments glowing in the night
As if she walked in paths of light.

I do not think life could bestow
A finer gift than loving toil,
The joy of helping things to grow,
Of working with the sun and soil.
That every soul you met and knew,
Was lovelier because of you.

POTTING SHED PALETTE
Jessie Walker Associates

My Favorite Easter Memory

Personal Stories of Treasured Memories from the Ideals Family of Readers

Wild Greens and Memories

When the sun grows warm and the long-slumbering earth wakes with wild plants, I remember my mother and the times she and I would go gathering wild greens. Our first trek over the fields in springtime was a treat to my winter-bound senses. The smell of fresh-plowed earth, the sound of the birds and brook, the feel of wind in my face—all were exciting heralds of a new season. Mother would gather a tin pail, a large knife for herself, and a smaller one for me. She would tie on her flowered gingham bonnet, I'd jerk on my worn winter cap, and we were off to the lower orchard.

The blue thistles were green and tender, just right for picking. Mother would stick her knife under the plant and cut off its roots. Then she'd lift it up and snip off the curly, dark green leaves. I'd do the same, except with my leaves there were usually bits of dry grass mixed in, which Mother would finger out.

She always said wild greens taste much better if you have different kinds in the pot, so we'd wander on to find tender white blossom and wild lettuce. After we'd found a few bunches of these, on we'd go, this time looking for lamb's-quarters, bunch greens, field cress, and spikes of shiny poke. Soon the pail was full and we walked back home.

I watched as Mother washed the greens carefully and then put them on the stove to boil.

"Always parboil wild greens," Mother would say. "My granny taught me that long ago. They don't taste so strong when you parboil them." She seasoned the greens well with salt and bacon grease and served them with a round pone of cornbread, which was baked from our own meal supply.

Time changes ways of living. Few people pick wild greens anymore. I do, but only in my memory. When the late snows melt and the new colors of spring begin to show, I skip off to the lower orchard. Mother isn't far behind with her tin pail and sharp knife, and once again we gather greens.

O. J. Robertson
Russell Springs, Kentucky

Editor's Note: If you wish to gather wild greens yourself, be sure you know which are safe and which can be harmful if ingested.

When Gals Wore Easter Bonnets

One of my favorite holiday memories is the outing to find the perfect Easter bonnet. When I was a little girl in the early 1950s, it became a tradition for my elderly neighbor Mary (who spoke with a thick Portuguese accent), my mother, and I to make a date to go shopping downtown for our Easter finery.

We would board the big bus for the long ride, which then cost all of twenty cents! I loved to

watch my dimes fall down the little collection box, and I would always sit up near the front so I could listen to the jingle of the coins as people boarded and the swish-swish noise of the doors. There was so much to take in during the ride. I loved to listen to Mary speak in her thick accent, and her smile was always so cheerful; it lit up her whole face. For years I thought she always had the hiccups in the morning, because she would often tell my mother, "When I hiccup in the morning . . ." Finally, I caught on that she meant *wake up*. As Mary and my mother chatted, I watched all the people get on and off the bus at the different stops. Some were nicely dressed, some young, some old, some poorly dressed, and occasionally there would be someone that seemed very strange.

We would get off in town, browse through a couple of shops, and usually end up doing all our serious shopping at Woolworth's and Capwell's. Mother and Mary would try on hat after hat while admiring themselves in the little round mirrors. After carefully making their selections, they would take me to the children's department, where I would usually get a new dress and always a new pair of shiny patent leather shoes, white frilly socks, white gloves, and, of course, my new Easter bonnet. I would always choose a colorful hat with a big, wide brim, as I thought it made me look just like a glamorous starlet.

My favorite part of the day was lunch, when Mary would treat us to lunch either at the Tea Room or Woolworth's counter. I chose the turkey and mashed potatoes special and felt like quite the young woman dining in style. For dessert, Mother and I would share an enormous banana split and Mary would order coffee and pie. Mother would leave some coins on the counter, and then it was time to start home.

Back on the bus with our shopping bags and full stomachs, the ladies' chatter and the swishing door would lull me to sleep against my mother's arm. Before I knew it, the ride would be over and Mother and Mary would call to me to wake up. I would rub my sleepy eyes, remembering all the excitement of the day and smiling at the thought of showing off my beautiful new Easter bonnet.

Sandy Alarcon
Twain Harte, California

Easter Morning Church Service

One of my cherished memories is of everyone in my family, regardless of their church affiliation, attending Mama's little rural church in Powell, Texas, on Easter morning. We were always a motley bunch and filled up a couple of pews. My brother was fresh from the cotton field and held the hymn book gingerly in his rough, toil-worn hands. His wife sat next to him, singing alto; not too melodiously but certainly loudly. My oldest sister missed part of the sermon as she rescued her two little boys from under the pew. Her daughters sat stiff with embarrassment at the antics of their brothers. Another sister sat prim and erect, not a hair out of place, as she cast side glances at her husband to be sure he didn't fall asleep. My two younger sisters, who were quite pretty, got admiring glances from many potential suitors who should have been looking at the preacher. And Mama, looking like an angel, *always* won the corsage for having family present from the greatest distance. Pride in family, love for one another, and praise of God all created that special ambience at our Easter morning church service of long ago.

Faye Field
Longview, Texas

Editor's Note: Do you have a special holiday or seasonal memory that you'd like to share with the Ideals family of readers? We'd love to read it! Send your typed memory to:

My Favorite Memory
c/o Editorial Department
Ideals Magazine
535 Metroplex Drive, Suite 250
Nashville, Tennessee 37211

April Melodies

Lon Myruski

Flirtatious April clouds furl round
Deep purple mountains high,
Embracing dearly ancient peaks
Amid a new springtide
As golden streams of sunlight prompt
Affectionate displays,
Caressing gently hoary crags
To kiss their snows away.

Beguiling April melodies
Borne sweetly on the breeze
Waft errantly o'er lea and wold,
Romancing blossomed trees.
And there I wander, captive to
The call of my heartstrings,
Infatuated helplessly
Beneath the spell of spring.

Woodland Symphony

Marie Rogers Altpeter

I hear sweet music borne on treble winds,
Staccato notes of woodland streams nearby;
I love to hear your earth-song symphony,
Look up at your cathedral, turquoise sky.
The violets nod in emerald pews of moss
While pastel flowers decked in gay attire
Sing joyously their Easter hymn today,
Accompanied by songbirds in the choir.

SOL DUC FALLS
Sol Duc Rainforest
Olympia National Park, Washington
Adam Jones Photography

Readers' Forum

Meet Our Ideals Readers and Their Families

The editors at Ideals are always looking for well-written, nostalgic reminiscences, especially about life on the farm. If you have a particular memory of the treasured days of yesteryear on the farm, send your typed manuscript to: NOSTALGIC REMINISCENCES, C/O EDITORIAL DEPARTMENT, IDEALS MAGAZINE, P.O. BOX 305300, NASHVILLE, TENNESSEE 37230.

Your privacy is important to us. From time to time we allow other companies, such as book clubs, to mail offers to our subscribers if we think the offer is appropriate. On occasion we also make offers to our subscribers by telephone to purchase Ideals books. If you would prefer not to receive either or both of these offers, please let us know by calling 1-800-558-4343 or writing to Customer Service Department, Ideals Publications Inc., P.O. Box 305300, Nashville, TN 37230.

Instead of candy, this Easter basket is filled with seven-month-old Hayden Elizabeth Murphy, great-granddaughter of LUCILLE HEADEN of Sulphur, Louisiana. Hayden (who was named after Lucille's family name) is the daughter of Todd and Patricia Murphy of Tuscaloosa, Alabama, and the granddaughter of Bonnie Murphy. Great-grandma Lucille tells us she is very proud of Hayden and her four other grandchildren.

THANK YOU Lucille Headen and Dorothy Jimison for sharing with *Ideals*. We hope to hear from other readers who would like to share photos and stories with the *Ideals* family. Please include a self-addressed, stamped envelope if you would like the photos returned. Keep your original photographs for safekeeping and send duplicate photos along with your name, address, and telephone number to:

READERS' FORUM
IDEALS PUBLICATIONS INC.
P.O. BOX 305300
NASHVILLE, TENNESSEE 37230

Publisher, Patricia A. Pingry
Editor, Lisa C. Ragan
Copy Editor, Michelle Prater Burke
Electronic Prepress Manager, Tina Wells Davenport
Contributing Editors,
Lansing Christman, Deana Deck, Pamela Kennedy,
Patrick McRae, Mary Skarmeas, Nancy Skarmeas

ACKNOWLEDGMENTS

WHEN ATTICS WERE IN STYLE from *LOVE AND LAUGHTER* by Marjorie Holmes. Copyright © 1967 by Marjorie Holmes Mighell. Used by permission of Doubleday, a division of Bantam Doubleday Dell Publishing Group, Inc. GARDEN MAGIC from *BESIDE STILL WATERS* by Edna Jaques, copyright © 1939 by Thomas Allen & Son, Limited. Reprinted by permission. EASTER IN NEW ENGLAND from *NEW ENGLAND HERITAGE AND OTHER POEMS* by Rose Koralewsky, copyright © 1949 by Bruce Humphries, Inc. Used by permission of Branden Publishing, Boston. A GARDEN from *MY HEART WAKETH* by Isla Paschal Richardson, copyright © 1947 by Bruce Humphries, Inc. Used by permission of Branden Publishing, Boston. Our sincere thanks to the following authors whom we were unable to contact: Mary Jeannette Bassett for REDBIRD ON A DOGWOOD TREE and May Smith White for SPRING'S RECURRING MAGIC.

DOROTHY JIMISON of Appomattox, Virginia, shares with us this photo of her two-year-old granddaughter Katie all dressed up and enjoying a field of beautiful bluebonnets. Each spring, the flowers brighten fields near Katie's home in Temple, Texas, where she lives with her younger sister, Lucy, and her parents, John and Victoria Jimison.

Dorothy, who received her first issue of *Ideals* as a Christmas gift in 1955, has treasured her copies for more than forty years.

Easter Morning

Kathleen R. Pawley

Oh, happy, blessed Easter morn,
Oh, day of faith and hope reborn,
How bright the day, how warm the sun
To cheer the hearts of everyone!
Is this the selfsame sun that shone
And glinted on the rolled-back stone?

How sweet the smell of spring's warm breeze
Now moving through the budding trees.
Were floral-scented breezes there
To stir His robe and touch His hair
When first He came forth from the tomb
As new life from a mother's womb?

How proud the yellow tulips grow
From bulbs that slept neath winter's snow.
Did hyacinth and crocus nod
Along the path that Mary trod?

The robin's voice now singing out
Shouts "Resurrection!" all about.
A sound more sweet than birdsong came
To Mary when He spoke her name.

In sun and flowers, birds and breeze—
His presence lives in such as these.
Oh, happy, joyful Easter morn;
New life, new faith, new hope are born!

UNITED STATES POSTAL SERVICE • REQUIRED BY 39 U.S.C. 3685 • STATEMENT OF OWNERSHIP, MANAGEMENT, AND CIRCULATION

1. Publication Title: Ideals. 2. Publication No. 0019-137X. 3. Filing Date: 10/1/96. 4. Issue Frequency: 8 times a year, February, March, May, June, August, September, November, and December. 5. No. of Issues Published Annually: Eight. 6. Annual Subscription Price: $19.95. 7. Complete Mailing Address of Known Office of Publication: 535 Metroplex Dr., Ste. 250, PO Box 305300, Davidson County, Nashville, TN 37230-5300. 8. Complete Mailing Address of Headquarters or General Business Office of Publisher: 535 Metroplex Dr., Ste. 250, PO Box 305300, Davidson County, Nashville, TN 37230-5300. 9. Full Names and Complete Addresses of Publisher, Editor, and Managing Editor. Publisher: Patricia A. Pingry, 535 Metroplex Dr., Ste. 250, Nashville, TN 37211; Editor: Lisa C. Ragan, 535 Metroplex Dr., Ste. 250, Nashville, TN 37211; Managing Editor: Lisa C. Ragan, 535 Metroplex Dr., Ste. 250, Nashville, TN 37211.10. Owner (Full Name and Complete Mailing Address): Ideals Publications Incorporated, 535 Metroplex Drive, Suite 250, Nashville, TN 37211. Stockholders Owning or Holding 1 Percent or More of Total Amount of Stock: Simon Waterlow, President, 535 Metroplex Drive, Suite 250, Nashville, TN 37211; Martin Flanagan, Vice President, Finance, 535 Metroplex Drive, Suite 250, Nashville, TN 37211; Patricia A. Pingry, Vice President, Publisher, 535 Metroplex Drive, Suite 250, Nashville, TN 37211. 11. Known Bondholders, Mortgagees, and Other Security Holders Owning or Holding 1 Percent or More of Total Amount of Bonds, Mortgages, or Other Securities: Egmont Foundation, Vognmagergade II, 1148 Copenhagen K., Denmark and Trans Financial Bank, PO Box 3490, Clarksville, TN 37043. 12. For completion by nonprofit organizations authorized to mail at special rates: Not Applicable. 13. Publication Name: Ideals. 14. Issue Date for Circulation Data Below: Friendship, September 1996. 15. Extent and Nature of Circulation: Average No. Copies Each Issue During Preceding 12 Months: A. Total No. Copies (Net Press Run): 199,297. Paid and/or Requested Circulation: B1. Sales Through Dealers and Carriers, Street Vendors, and Counter Sales: 29,493. B2. Paid or Requested Mail Subscriptions: 150,849. C. Total Paid and/or Requested Circulation: 180,342. D. Free Distribution by Mail: 0. E. Free Distribution Outside the Mail: 0. F. Total Free Distribution: 0. G. Total Distribution: 180,342. H. Copies Not Distributed: (1) Office Use, Leftovers, Spoiled: 8,632. (2) Return from News Agents: 10,323. I. Total: 199,297. Percent Paid and/or Requested Circulation: 100%. Average No. Copies of Single Issue Published Nearest to Filing Date: A. Total No. Copies (Net Press Run): 153,579. Paid and/or Requested Circulation: B1. Sales Through Dealers and Carriers, Street Vendors, and Counter Sales: 4,636. B2. Paid or Requested Mail Subscriptions: 140,703. C. Total Paid and/or Requested Circulation: 145,339. D. Free Distribution by Mail: 0. E. Free Distribution Outside the Mail: 0. F. Total Free Distribution: 0. G. Total Distribution: 145,339. H. Copies Not Distributed: (1) Office Use, Leftovers, Spoiled: 8,162. (2) Return from News Agents: 78. I. Total: 153,579. Percent Paid and/or Requested Circulation: 100%.

I certify that all information furnished is true and complete.
Rose A. Yates, Vice President, Direct Marketing Systems and Operations

A timeless collection of paintings, poems, and prose that celebrates the joys and rewards of being and having a friend . . .

The Gift of Friendship

The pages of this book capture the true meaning of friendship in words and images that will inspire and uplift you.

You are invited to examine *The Gift of Friendship* free for 30 days—and to order additional copies as gifts for your closest friends, if you wish. When your copy arrives, take some time to explore this celebration of the yearning for closeness and "connectedness" that begins in childhood . . .

Scuffing through gutterways the fallen leaves yet, with a need they do not understand,
Once in a while they take each other's hand.

Sarah Litsey

and continues long into the golden years of our lives . . .

And when beyond the distant hills
The golden sun of life descends,
We find God's greatest gift has been
The love of true and faithful friends.

Patience Strong

Warm and Heartfelt Poems about Friends . . . You'll find beautiful verse from the pens of the famous—from Patience Strong to Edgar Guest to Ralph Waldo Emerson as well as moving poems by unknown authors.

Exquisite Paintings and Photographs Bathed in the Light of Friendship . . . Here are fine paintings that evoke the spirit of friendship with paint, canvas, and delicate watercolor.

Letters Between Famous Friends . . . From Helen Keller to her teacher Annie Sullivan . . . from composer Richard Rodgers to lyricist Oscar Hammerstein and more.

Essays and Writings about the Blessings of Friendship . . . Ella Wheeler Wilcox wrote: "Friends—and the word means much— / So few there are who reach like thee . . . hand give the clasp, when most its need is felt, / Friend, newly found, accept my full heart's thanks."

"Do not keep the alabaster boxes of your love and tenderness sealed until your friends are dead. Fill their lives with sweetness. Speak approving, cheering words while their ears can hear them and while their hearts can be thrilled by them."

Henry Ward Beecher

INCLUDES FREE Mystery Gift!

In order to do justice to the many examples of fine art and to the delicate typefaces of the text, only the finest materials and printing techniques have been employed in the production of *The Gift of Friendship*; and the book is case-bound with high gloss lamination that draws out the subtle hues and tones of the truly magnificent painting "In the Orchard" by Henry Hubert La Thangue that is reproduced on the cover.

No need to send money now . . . simply return your Certificate for a 30-day free examination!

MAIL TODAY TO: Ideals Publications, Inc., PO Box 305300, Nashville, TN 37230

FREE EXAMINATION CERTIFICATE

❑ **YES!** I'd like to examine *The Gift of Friendship* for 30 days free. If after a month I am not delighted with it, I may return it and owe nothing. If I decide to keep it, I will be billed $19.95 plus shipping and handling. In either case, the FREE Mystery Gift is mine to keep.

Please print your name and address:

MY NAME

MY ADDRESS

CITY   STATE   ZIP
Do you wish a copy for yourself? ❑ Yes   ❑ No   For Gift Copies Complete Below:

Gift Name _____   Gift Name _____

Address _____   Address _____

City _____ State ___ ZIP _____   City _____ State ___ ZIP _____

❑ Please Bill Me ❑ Charge My: ❑ MasterCard ❑ Visa ❑ Diners ❑ Discover

Expiration Date: _____

Signature _____

Orders subject to acceptance. We regret that we cannot process orders from outside the U.S. BD 000

"Blessed are they," wrote Thomas Hughes, Victorian writer and philanthropist, "who have the gift of making friends."

The Gift of Friendship

Yours for a 30-day free examination . . . simply return your Free Examination Certificate today.

Faithful Friends . . . Celebrate the loyalty of friendship in pictures and in words such as those from Kipling's The Thousandth Man: "One man in a thousand, Solomon says, / Will stick more close than a brother."

The Inspiration of Friendship . . . Celebrate the inspirational power of friendship: "The children of the Lord, are they," wrote Henry van Dyke, "And as they come and go, / There is not one among them all that is not good to know."

Friends in Nature . . . Celebrate friendship between human beings and the natural world with quiet thoughts such as those of William Wordsworth:

"In this sequestered nook how sweet / To sit upon my orchard seat, / And birds and flowers once more to greet, / My last year's friends together."

Letters between Friends . . . Celebrate historic records of great friendships—as in the letter from Richard Wagner to Franz Liszt that closed with the words: "It is noble to have a friend, but still nobler to be a friend."

Friends of Childhood . . . Celebrate the natural spontaneity evoked by Edgar A. Guest:

"When some scrubby yellow dog needs sympathy and joy, / He's certain of a friend in need, if he can find a boy."

Famous Friends . . . Celebrate the power of friendship as a moving force in the lives of famous people. Helen Keller wrote of ". . . invisible lines stretched between my spirit and the spirits of others."

Familiar Friends . . . Celebrate the instant recognition of friendship's comfortable familiarity, as expressed by James J. Metcalfe: "The world is filled with friendly things / For those who try to find them."

160 pages of heavy enamel paper with laminated, full color cover

INCLUDES **FREE** Mystery Gift!

COMPLETE THE FORM ON THE REVERSE SIDE NOW TO ORDER THIS EXTRAORDINARY IDEALS VOLUME

The Gift of Friendship

FOR

30 DAYS FREE!